ICH PUTZE MEINE ZÄHNE GERN
I LOVE TO BRUSH MY TEETH

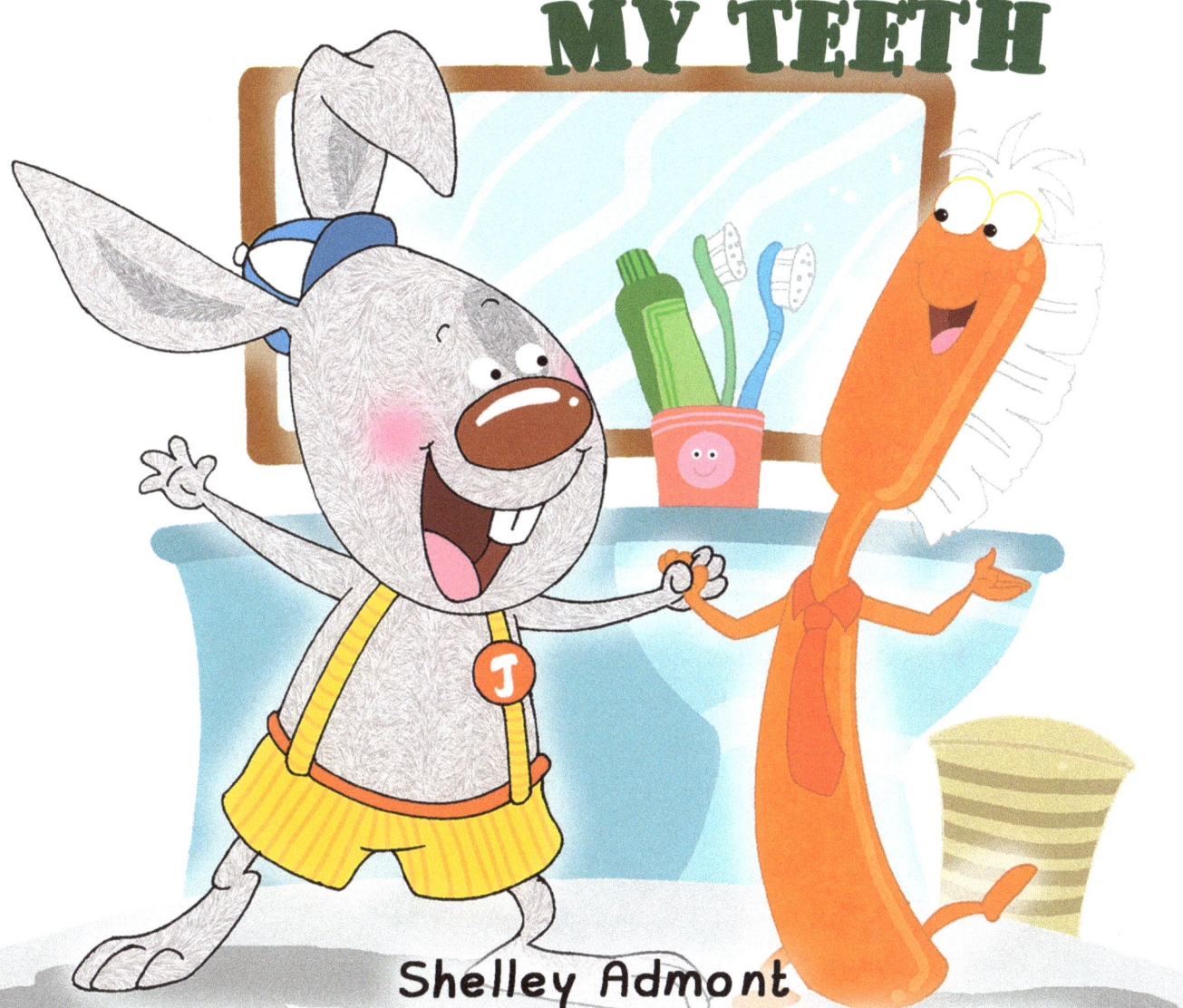

Shelley Admont
Illustriert von Sonal Goyal und Sumit Sakhuja

www.sachildrensbooks.com

Copyright©2014 by Inna Nusinsky Shmuilov
innans@gmail.com

All rights reserved. No part of this book may be reproduced in any form or by any electronic or mechanical means, including information storage and retrieval systems, without written permission from the publisher or author, except in the case of a reviewer, who may quote brief passages embodied in critical articles or in a review.

Alle Rechte vorbehalten. Kein Teil dieses Buches darf in irgendeiner Form oder durch irgendwelche elektronischen oder mechanischen Mitteln, einschließlich Informationen Regalbediengeräte schriftlich beim Verlag, mit Ausnahme von einem Rezensenten, kurze Passagen in einer Bewertung zitieren darf reproduziert, ohne Erlaubnis.

First edition, 2015
Translated from English by Tess Parthum
Aus dem Englischen übersetzt von Tess Parthum

I love to brush my teeth (German Bilingual Edition)/ Shelley Admont
ISBN: 978-1-77268-073-7 paperback
ISBN: 978-1-77268-614-2 hardcover
ISBN: 978-1-77268-074-4 ebook

Although the author and the publisher have made every effort to ensure the accuracy and completeness of information contained in this book, we assume no responsibility for errors , inaccuracies, omission, inconsistency, or consequences from such information.

Please note that the German and English versions of the story have been written to be as close as possible. However, in some cases they differ in order to accommodate nuances and fluidity of each language.

für die, die ich am meisten liebe–S.A.

For those I love the most– S.A.

Der Morgen kam und die Sonne schien im weit entfernten Wald. Dort, in einem kleinen Haus, lebte der kleine Hase Jimmy mit seinen Eltern und zwei älteren Brüdern.

Morning came and the sun was shining in the faraway forest. There, in a small house, lived little bunny Jimmy, with his parents and two older brothers.

Mama kam ins Zimmer, das Jimmy mit seinen Brüdern teilte.

Mom came into the room that Jimmy shared with his brothers.

Zuerst küsste sie den ältesten Bruder, der friedlich in seinem blauen Bett schlief.

First she kissed the oldest brother, who slept peacefully in his blue bed.

Dann gab sie dem mittleren Bruder einen Kuss. Er schlief noch in seinem grünen Bett.

Next she gave a kiss to the middle brother. He was still sleeping in his green bed.

Schließlich ging die Mama zu Jimmys orangefarbenem Bett und gab ihm einen Kuss.

Finally, Mom went to Jimmy's orange bed, and gave him a kiss.

„Guten Morgen, Kinder", sagte Mama. „Es ist Zeit, aufzustehen."

"Good morning, children," said Mom. "It's time to rise."

Der älteste Bruder stieg aus dem Bett und ging ins Bad.

Getting out of bed, the oldest brother made his way to the bathroom.

„Wow!", rief er, „Ich habe eine brandneue Zahnbürste! Sie ist blau, meine Lieblingsfarbe. Danke, Mama." Er begann, seine Zähne zu putzen.

"Wow!" he shouted, "I have a brand-new toothbrush! It's blue, my favorite color. Thank you, Mom." He started to brush his teeth.

Der mittlere Bruder folgte ihm. „Ich habe auch eine neue Zahnbürste und meine ist grün!", rief er und fing ebenfalls an, seine Zähne zu putzen.

The middle brother followed him. "I have a new toothbrush as well, and mine's green!" he exclaimed and also began to brush his teeth.

Jimmy kletterte aus dem Bett und lief langsam zum Badezimmer. Warum soll ich mir überhaupt die Mühe machen, meine Zähne zu putzen? dachte er. Meine Zähne sind gut so, wie sie sind.

Jimmy got out of bed and walked slowly towards the bathroom. *Why even bother brushing my teeth?* he thought. *My teeth are fine as they are.*

„Schau, Jimmy", sagte sein ältester Bruder, „du hast auch eine neue Zahnbürste. Sie ist orange, wie dein Bett."

"Look, Jimmy," said his oldest brother, "you have a new toothbrush too. It's orange like your bed."

„Dann habe ich eben eine neue Zahnbürste, na und?" Jimmy stand vor dem Spiegel, aber er fing immer noch nicht an, seine Zähne zu putzen.

"So I have a new toothbrush, big deal." Jimmy stood in front of the mirror, but he still didn't start brushing his teeth.

„Kinder, beeilt euch, das Frühstück ist fast fertig", hörten sie die leise Stimme ihrer Mutter. „Sind alle fertig mit dem Zähneputzen?"

"Kids, hurry up! Breakfast is almost ready," they heard their mother's soft voice. "Has everyone finished brushing their teeth?"

„Ich bin fertig", antwortete der älteste Bruder und rannte aus dem Bad.

"I've finished," answered the oldest brother and ran out of the bathroom.

„Ich auch", erwiderte der mittlere Bruder. Er rannte seinem Bruder hinterher in die Küche.

"Me too," replied the middle brother. He ran after his brother to the kitchen.

„Mama, ich bin auch fertig mit dem Zähneputzen", rief Jimmy. Er war gerade dabei, aus dem Badezimmer zu gehen, als er eine Stimme hörte.

"Mom, I finished brushing my teeth too," shouted Jimmy. He was just about to leave the bathroom, when he heard a voice.

„Es ist nicht nett zu lügen", sagte die Stimme. „Du hast deine Zähne nicht geputzt."

"It's not nice to lie," the voice said. "You didn't brush your teeth."

„Wer hat das gesagt?", fragte Jimmy, während er verwirrt umherblickte.
„Hier drüben", kam die Antwort.

"Who said that?" asked Jimmy as he looked around in confusion.
"Over here," was the reply.

Seine neue orange Zahnbürste stand auf dem Waschbecken und sah ihn schräg an.

Frowning at him was his new orange toothbrush, standing on the counter.

„Eine Zahnbürste kann nicht sprechen", sagte er mit erstaunter Stimme.

"A toothbrush can't talk," he said in a stunned voice.

„Kann ich wohl. Ich bin eine magische Zahnbürste", sagte die Zahnbürste stolz. „Meine Aufgabe ist es, sicherzustellen, dass JEDER seine Zähne putzt."

"I sure can. I'm a magical toothbrush," said the toothbrush proudly. "My job is to make sure EVERYONE brushes his teeth."

Jimmy antwortete mit einem Lachen: „Ich habe meine Zähne nicht geputzt und nichts Schlimmes ist mir passiert."

Jimmy laughed in response. "I didn't brush my teeth and nothing bad happened to me."

„Schau dich selbst an", sagte die Bürste. „Deine Zähne sind gelb und dein Atem riecht schrecklich."

"Look at yourself," the brush said. "Your teeth are yellow and your breath smells terrible."

„Das ist nicht wahr, Bürste, das denkst du dir nur aus!" Jimmy nahm die Zahnbürste und warf sie in die Badezimmerecke.

"That's not true, brush. You're just making it up!" Jimmy took the toothbrush and threw it far into the corner of the bathroom.

Dann rannte er in die Küche, um zu frühstücken.

Then he ran into the kitchen to have his breakfast.

„Das ist keine Art, mich zu behandeln", schrie die Zahnbürste. „Ich bin eine magische Zahnbürste. Ich werde dir beweisen, wie wichtig ich bin!"

"That's no way to treat me," shouted the toothbrush. "I'm a magical toothbrush. I'll prove how important I am!"

Jimmy setzte sich währenddessen bereits neben seine Brüder in der Küche.

By this time, Jimmy was already sitting down next to his brothers in the kitchen.

Er nahm ein Sandwich und wollte hineinbeißen. Doch da sprang das Sandwich aus Jimmys Händen direkt auf den Teller seines ältesten Bruders.

He took a sandwich and brought it to his mouth. But then the sandwich jumped out of Jimmy's hands right onto the plate of his oldest brother.

Anstatt in sein Sandwich, hatte Jimmy in seine Finger gebissen - fest!
„Autsch, das tut weh!", schrie er.

Instead of the sandwich, Jimmy had bitten his fingers — hard!
"Ouch, it hurts!" he yelled.

„Wem gehört dieses Sandwich?", fragte der ältere Bruder.

"Who does this sandwich belong to?" the brother asked.

„Das ist mein Sandwich", antwortete Jimmy. „Es ist vor mir weggelaufen!"

"My sandwich ran away from me," answered Jimmy. "It's mine!"

„Du hast aber eine blühende Fantasie, Liebling. Wie kann ein Sandwich weglaufen?", sagte seine Mutter.

"Quite an imagination you have, sweetie. How can a sandwich run away?" his mother said.

„Ich weiß es nicht! Aber es ist wirklich weggelaufen", sagte Jimmy.

"I don't know how, but that's really what happened," said Jimmy.

Dann gab ihm die Mama einen großen Teller voll Salat. „Hier, vielleicht möchtest du stattdessen lieber einen leckeren Gemüsesalat essen", sagte sie.

Then, Mom gave him a big plate full of salad. "Here, perhaps you would like to eat a delicious vegetable salad instead," she said.

„Lecker, ich liebe Gemüsesalat", sagte Jimmy und wollte anfangen zu essen. Plötzlich sprang der Salatteller auf und landete auf dem Tisch bei seinem mittleren Bruder.

"Yummy, I love vegetable salad," said Jimmy, about to start eating. Suddenly, the salad plate leaped up and settled down on the table near his middle brother.

„Schau", sagte der mittlere Bruder, „wie ist dein Teller hier hingekommen?"

"Look," said the middle brother, "how did your plate get over here?"

„Du hattest Recht, Schatz! Dein Essen rennt vor dir weg!", sagte ihre erstaunte Mama. „Das ist merkwürdig."

"You were right, honey! Your food is running away from you!" said their astonished mom. "That's strange."

„Mama, ich bekomme wirklich Hunger. Was kann ich essen?", fragte Jimmy.

"Mom, I'm getting hungry already. What can I eat?" said Jimmy.

Mama dachte einen Moment nach. „Wie wäre es mit deinem Lieblingskarottenkuchen? Ich werde dir ein großes Stück geben."

Mom thought for a moment. "How about your favorite carrot cake? I'll give you a big slice."

„Oh ja, Karottenkuchen! Den liebe ich so sehr", rief Jimmy glücklich, „Danke, Mama."

"Oh yes, carrot cake! I love it so much," Jimmy shouted happily, "Thanks, Mom."

Bevor Jimmy allerdings den Kuchen nehmen konnte, begann dieser, in der Luft zu schweben. Er flog ins Wohnzimmer und landete auf der Couch.

However, before Jimmy could take the cake, it began to float in the air. It flew into the living room and settled on the couch.

Jimmy hüpfte von seinem Stuhl und begann, das Kuchenstück zu jagen. Er sprang auf das Sofa, aber der Kuchen sauste zurück zum Tisch.

Jimmy hopped out of his chair and started chasing the piece of cake. He jumped on the sofa, but the cake zoomed back to the table.

Jimmy rannte zum Tisch zurück, aber der Kuchen flog aus dem Haus. Der Kuchen flog um das Haus herum, während Jimmy ihm folgte.

Jimmy ran back to the table and then the cake flew out of the house. Jimmy rushed after it. The cake looped around the house while Jimmy trailed behind it.

Eine Runde, und noch eine Runde, und Jimmy verfolgte ihn noch immer.

Another round and another and another, and still Jimmy followed.

Bis er außer Atem war. Müde setzte sich Jimmy in den Hauseingang und fing an zu weinen.

Until he had run out of breath. Tired, Jimmy sat down at the entrance of the house and started crying.

Im gleichen Moment kamen zwei seiner Freunde vorbei.

At the same moment, two of his friends were passing by.

„Hey, Jimmy", begrüßten sie ihn. „Warum sitzt du hier und siehst so traurig aus? Komm, spiel mit uns."

"Hey, Jimmy," they greeted. "Why are you sitting here looking so sad? Come play with us."

„Ja, das würde ich gern!" Jimmy rannte ihnen entgegen. „Ihr werdet nicht glauben, was mir heute passiert ist!"

"Yes, I'd like that!" Jimmy ran towards them. "You won't believe what happened to me today!"

Aber als er seinen Mund öffnete, riefen seine Freunde: „Igitt, was für ein Gestank! Wir werden woanders spielen gehen, während du deine Zähne putzen gehst!" Damit rannten sie weg.

But, as he opened his mouth, the friends shouted, "Yikes, what a stink! We'll go play somewhere else while you go brush your teeth!"
With that, they ran away.

Jimmy brach erneut in Tränen aus und ging ins Haus. Er lief ins Badezimmer und sah die magische Zahnbürste in der Luft fliegen. Sie lächelte ihn freundlich an.

Bursting into tears yet again, Jimmy entered the house. He went to the bathroom and saw the magical toothbrush flying in the air, smiling kindly at him.

„Hallo, Jimmy. Ich habe auf dich gewartet. Möchtest du jetzt deine Zähne putzen?" Jimmy nickte.

"Hello, Jimmy. I've been waiting for you. Do you want to brush your teeth now?" Jimmy nodded.

Jimmy fing an, seine Zähne zu putzen. Von einer Seite zur anderen, oben und unten, vorne und hinten.

Jimmy started brushing his teeth, from one side to the other, top and bottom, front and back.

Jimmy blickte stolz sein Spiegelbild an und sagte: „Danke, Bürste. Es war sogar schön und angenehm, meine Zähne zu putzen. Jetzt habe ich auch einen frischen Atem."

Gazing proudly at his reflection in the mirror, Jimmy said, "Thank you, brush. It was even nice and pleasant to brush my teeth. I now have sweet-smelling breath too."

„Du siehst toll aus", sagte die Bürste. „Übrigens, mein Name ist Leah. Ich bin immer hier, um zu helfen."

"You look great," said the brush. "By the way, my name is Leah. I'm always here to help."

So wurden Jimmy und Leah gute Freunde.

That's how Jimmy and Leah became good friends.

Seit diesem Tag sehen sie sich täglich zweimal, um Jimmys Zähne zu schützen und ihnen dabei zu helfen, kräftig und gesund zu wachsen.

Ever since that day, they've seen each other twice a day to protect Jimmy's teeth and help them grow strong and healthy.

www.ingramcontent.com/pod-product-compliance
Lightning Source LLC
Chambersburg PA
CBHW051301110526
44589CB00025B/2902